Mrs. Christy's Bridge Party

(Sara Ware Bassett)

Mrs. Reginald Norman walked into Sherry's and sank down at a small table with the calm assurance of one conscious of being both beautiful and perfectly gowned. There were no defects for the critical world to take up and magnify. Her gown fitted flawlessly, was built by the highest court of appeal on Parisian fashions, and suited her to perfection.

There is nothing like such a latent consciousness to impart poise to the wearer. Dainty little Ethel Danielson followed, dropping into the opposite chair.

"It was awfully nice of you to set this time for me to meet and lunch with you," said Mrs. Danielson, leisurely drawing off her long gloves. "Really, if you do not set definite hours you never see your friends at all; this last whirl before Lent has been frightful, hasn't it? I'm worn to a shred!"

"Yes, I shall be glad of a rest. You must go to things--if for no other reason than to prove you are asked. I haven't seen any of my family for over a week. I saw your husband a moment or two at the Opera last night with the Goodhue Livingstons," returned Mrs. Norman, as she loosened her veil.

"Oh, did you? Poor Harry--how was he? He has been having the grip or something, his valet told me a couple of days ago," answered Mrs. Danielson carelessly. "Well, my dear, to change the subject--are you going to the Christy's bridge party? I'm simply dying of curiosity to know! I thought of you the minute I opened the cards and wondered what you would do--you have said so much about them."

"Don't mention bridge to me!" burst out Mrs. Norman emphatically. "Look at my hair--did you ever behold such a vision in your life? The parlor-maid did it, after much persuasion and an ample tip. I'm perfectly discouraged--Thérése has gone!"

"Gone? That maid you brought from Paris! Why you told me that nothing but fire or the sword would separate you from that girl," ejaculated Mrs. Danielson in surprise; "wasn't she satisfactory after all?"

"Perfectly satisfactory--perfectly, my love. I never had a maid who so thoroughly understood my style and what I could and could not wear. I was forced to let her go; every one of the eleven servants would have left. The housekeeper told me it was policy to dismiss her," said Mrs. Norman, thrusting her fork into a soft shell crab with great vehemence.

"Might one ask why they objected to her? Certainly, her nationality wasn't a ground for such a demand, for half your servants are French, aren't they?" questioned Mrs. Danielson with much interest.

"Oh, it wasn't that. She didn't play bridge! She just made the twelfth one, and her not playing spoiled the third table--they would not have her," explained Mrs. Norman dubiously.

"What are we coming to!" Mrs. Danielson exclaimed in despair; "I don't wonder you're discouraged--you have to be so careful how you are gotten up. You look so stunning in some things and so--well, you understand--one must study one's style! Now tell me, what are you going to do about the Christy's bridge? Everyone is wild over it! I've heard nothing else for days--it's to be quite the event of the season. Shall you go?"

"No. I have thought it all out. It seems to me some of us must take a stand. If we accept invitations from the Christys' why the harm is done--they will be in society before we know it! There are enough queer people in our set already without adding them. I shall not go!" Mrs. Norman drew herself up haughtily.

"That's just what I think," echoed Ethel Danielson; "we must, as you say, take some definite position in the matter. If we stand out I am sure others will. The Christys are simply dying to get in, and they have loads of money to back them. What was it--blacking? Something disagreeable, I remember."

"No, ink! Just as black and disgusting.

They've squandered hundreds on this bridge party; all the prizes were bought abroad, I hear, and Kathryn Van Rensselaer told me there were to be fifty tables," continued Mrs. Norman.

"It will be one of those horribly vulgar affairs with five times as much of everything as there is any need of, I suppose," rejoined Ethel scornfully.

"Do you know, I hear that ballroom is the most magnificent in New York--done entirely by Garten-Veen."

"Well, we shall at least hear about it," sighed Mrs. Norman, with a slight tinge of regret in her tone, "we'll telephone--you have one of course!"

"Have a telephone? Well, I should say! One might as well be out of the world as try to live without one. Everyone has one now," answered Mrs. Danielson with a shrug.

"Then do call me up and tell me everything you hear," said Mrs. Norman eagerly, "and I will call you. Thank Heaven, there are two of us with conscience enough to block the Christys' social pathway!"

During the week preceding the much talked of function, one heard it on every hand. Some said the prizes alone mounted up into the hundreds; others announced that the decorations were to be the floral marvel of the season; two reporters had been permitted to view Mrs. Christy's gown and wrote exhaustive descriptions on this monument to the Parisian art.

Mrs. Norman and Ethel Danielson had frequent long gossips over the telephone, relating each fresh item and exulting that they, at least, had not lost their heads.

"Elise Thayer says she shall not go if we don't," called Mrs. Norman with great satisfaction; "I have talked to her very seriously about it and told her it was her duty to the rest of us to stay away, and she says she will. No, I haven't sent regrets yet--I shall wait until the last moment and be as nasty as I can," and Mrs. Norman gave a rippling laugh.

At last the eventful day of the great bridge party came and among the early arriving guests was Mrs. Norman. She glanced around her, noting critically every detail of the luxurious house with its exquisite appointments. Of course Ethel Danielson and Elise Thayer would hear that she had come and be furious, but she was well prepared with explanations when next she should meet them. She had planned it all very carefully.

She was sweeping down the staircase to greet her hostess when she suddenly stopped aghast! From opposite directions--entirely unconscious of the other's approach--came Ethel Danielson and Elise Thayer. There was no avoiding the collision at the foot of the stairs and the three women were brought abruptly face to face.

"Mrs. Danielson!"

"Elise Thayer!"

"My dear Mrs. Norman!"

Mrs. Norman was the first to speak. She was the only one who had had the opportunity to summon her story to her tongue's end. She began glibly and with nervous haste:

"My dears, I positively had to come!

Reggie would have it so. He and Mr. Christy are mixed up in some financial operations, and he said it was policy: I'm perfectly mortified to be here!"

Nevertheless, she glanced about her in most interested scrutiny.

"It was a pure and simple case of money with me," announced Ethel Danielson, with suave frankness. "My furs are not paid for, and the bills for my Palm Beach gowns are pouring in. These trades people are so loathsomely prompt with their bills and so maddeningly slow every other way! I wish they would reverse it. So I came to see if I could not get something out of it--that's between us. If I draw any decent partners I ought to, for I generally have good luck."

"Now, Elise, you see we were each forced into coming," said Mrs. Norman accusingly, "for goodness sake, why did you come?"

"Well, I considered it carefully. The Christys are bound to get in--if not now, later! They have come to stay, and they will hammer away, with their millions behind them, until they're in. What's the use of standing out against it? They will only snub me by and by," returned Elise Thayer with defiant truthfulness.

Mrs. Norman colored and looked uneasily at Ethel Danielson.

Mrs. Danielson eyed Mrs. Norman uncomfortably. Each seemed to hear a fearless echo of her own secret reasoning.

"Besides," continued Elise, smiling honestly, "you know you each meant to come all the time, only you won't admit it."

For an instant there was an awkward pause, then Mrs. Norman laughed in chagrined amusement.

"Well, we won't discuss it now," she said; "run along up and leave your wraps--both of you--and I'll wait for you. We will go in together."

A few seconds later they were approaching their hostess with outstretched hands.

"My dear Mrs. Christy," cooed Mrs. Norman, "so good of you to include me among your guests! I know how many friends you have and one can't invite them all."

Mrs. Christy took the extended hand murmuring:

"So nice of you to come with your

chaos of engagements! Mrs. Danielson, too!"

"I was delighted to have you think of me, Mrs. Christy," Mrs. Danielson returned effusively, "and you may be sure yours was the only invitation I considered for this afternoon--I let all the others go."

Elise Thayer followed with:

"Mrs. Christy, I've so anticipated to-day! I adore bridge and to have the pleasure of being one of your guests made it additionally delightful."

The three moved on and glanced over the rapidly crowding rooms.

"Really," whispered Mrs. Norman, "everybody is here. I'm amazed! There are the Baring De Wolfs and the Wilson Delafields and Mrs. Morgan

Knickerbocker. You know how exclusive they are! And there is Mrs. Cecil Jerome! I saw her yesterday and she never said a word about coming."

"Let's go and speak to her a moment before they sit down to play," suggested Ethel Danielson.

As they drifted in and out of the gathering assembly, varied snatches of conversation reached them:

"Beautiful house, isn't it?"

"Yes, but overloaded--like the owner's hats! She is awfully bothered about getting hats, she told me, and recently a French milliner begged to see 'WHAT SHE COULD DO WITH HER.' Judging from the hat Mrs. Christy wore at the St. Regis the other day, I guess the woman found out! Any milliner who can get a patron to step out of the solitude of her boudoir in such a concoction must have convinced herself that she can do ANYTHING with her!"

"I don't think much of her gown," murmured another, "hideously unbecoming!"

"I hope we shall not run into any of those people who 'TAKE A HAND JUST TO ACCOMMODATE!'" chimed another. "I think there ought to be a law prohibiting women who haven't taken lessons in the game, going to parties and helping lose other people's money for them."

"I hate to play with either of those Hartwells--they simply blow your head off after every hand; they haven't any manners!" put in a blond in a creation of blue chiffon and silver.

"That girl in white over there ought to be ruled out!" said another guest. "She is that artist visiting the Hollingsworths. She made it HEARTS when I played with her once, 'so to lose as little as possible,' she said."

The calling of the game cut short further comments.

The company was seated, the hands dealt, and the great bridge party was at last really under way.

"Are they starting? I hope people won't talk--I don't think it's fair. Is it my make? I haven't a thing! I'll pass it. CLUBS! Heavens! I could have done better than that myself! What on earth did you have in your hand? I don't care what Elwell says--I don't think that's enough; of course we couldn't make it on that hand! It seems a shame to THROW points away. I am NOT angry--do you think I mind a few dollars? it's only so unnecessary! How many hands do we have to play with each partner? I never said I wanted to get rid of you. No, it's NOT the same thing--I simply asked!"

So the game went on!

Flushed cheeks and glistening eyes were the only indications that much was at stake; social veneer concealed the real anxiety of the players, but a hush of nervous tension pervaded the room. It was a relief when the last hand was concluded. Everyone crowded around the table where the beautiful prizes were displayed and where the scores were read.

"You don't mean to tell me that that girl who came with the Hollingsworths and can't play at all, has first choice!" whispered Mrs. Norman.

"A case of fool's luck, I guess," replied Mrs. Danielson, "let's see what she takes."

"LOOK! She's going to take that Tiffany glass vase when she might have had that diamond bracelet--probably thinks they are rhinestones!" burst out Elise Thayer.

"Prizes never go to the best players," said Mrs. Cecil Jerome in disgust. "It is never really fair."

Mrs. Cecil Jerome was conceded to be one of the "best players."

After the prizes had been duly admired and the winners congratulated, the throng of exquisitely gowned women flocked about the little gilt tables in the dining-room, chatting eagerly and comparing scores.

[Illustration: "*The throng of exquisitely gowned women flocked about the little gilt tables in the dining-room.*"]

Mrs. Christy flitted among her guests with a smile and cordial word for each, but to some favored few she devoted her especial attention. She stopped beside one group in the corner of the dining-room more than once.

"Your dining-room is so attractive, Mrs. Christy," said Mrs. Norman, as her hostess sat down beside her for an instant.

"It is good of you to say so--you do things so exquisitely yourself that I'm quite afraid of YOU," returned Mrs. Christy with disarming frankness.

She glanced at Miss Thayer, Mrs. Danielson and Mrs. Cecil Jerome, who were also at the table.

"You clever people," she went on, "must be my guides, for New York is rather new to me--we have lived West so much. You are all such authorities on social matters that I shall have to depend on you for many things. You'll help me, won't you?"

What women could resist such delicate flattery?

The four smiled graciously.

"Tell me, Mrs. Danielson," Mrs. Christy continued, "are you going to Newport this summer--or haven't you decided?"

"Oh, we've decided! We've rented our house and we intend to spend the summer in Switzerland and the Tyrol," answered Mrs. Danielson. "What are you going to do, Mrs. Christy?"

"Jack and I expect to take an automobile trip through England and Scotland--if he can get away," returned Mrs. Christy, "and by the way, what do you all do with your houses through the summer months? That is bothering me now! Do you leave your servants in them all summer?"

"Oh, no," exclaimed Mrs. Danielson hastily, "we have had such frightful experiences doing that! One summer we had fine servants and we wanted to hold on to them so we kept them in the house all the time we were gone and we hadn't been back any time at all before they left in a body! So pleasant to feel you'd only been giving a house-party for them!" she concluded sarcastically.

"Why my dear, our servants had a dance in our house!" put in Mrs. Norman.

"I always put a care-taker in ours," said Miss Thayer.

"Don't have a care-taker!" burst out Mrs. Cecil Jerome. "While our care-taker was living in the basement, burglars got through our scuttle and robbed all the upper part of the house!"

"You make a great mistake," said Mrs. Danielson.

"Don't you know about the Holmes Company? They have wired our house every year since that experience with our servants--why, it's ten years now! It is the only way to leave your house during the summer." I heard the other day, said a handsome woman joining the group, "that, that company had opened offices of their own all through the city this year and they will not hereafter connect houses with the District Telegraph offices, so you see their service is going to be a hundred per cent. better than it has ever been before."

"You better wire your house, Mrs. Christy," said Mrs. Danielson, "you'll feel perfectly safe then. An awfully funny thing happened to me when ours was first done! Mr. Danielson neglected to have my signature on the coupon and I came up from Newport and couldn't get into my own house! I was raging at the time, but when I thought it over afterward it convinced me how secure the protection is."

"Was it really true that your care-taker took boarders in your house while you were in Europe a few years ago," asked Mrs. Norman, turning to a newcomer who had joined them.

"Yes, we had it wired the minute we found it out. It put a stop to that sort of thing!" returned the woman emphatically.

"I never heard of such things!" gasped Mrs. Christy.

"I didn't know they would dare!"

"Dare? They dare anything!" snapped a tall girl in green.

"Well, I shall have it wired the instant we go," said Mrs. Christy conclusively. "I did not know there was any company who did that sort of thing. I am perfectly relieved to solve the problem!"

She went on into the drawing-room and the groups of guests at the tables gradually broke up and followed making their adieux.

The instant Mrs. Reginald Norman reached home she called Mrs.

Danielson up on the telephone.

"What did you think of it, Ethel?" she asked eagerly.

"It was a lovely party! All in such good taste, didn't you think so?" returned Ethel Danielson. "Mrs. Christy, too, made a much better appearance than I expected. She has a good deal of SAVOIR FAIRE already!"

"Yes, and she'll gain more as time goes on," replied Mrs. Norman. "How do you suppose she ever got the Schermerhorn's and the De Witts there."

"I can't imagine and it doesn't make much difference now, how she did it! I got my furs paid for which pleased me into the ground. Wouldn't we have been idiots to stay away? We should never have forgiven ourselves for from now on, Mrs. Christy is unquestionably IN SOCIETY. She has 'bridged it' in more senses than one!"

THE END